Look What I Found!

By the Pond

W
FRANKLIN
LONDON•SY

First published in 2005 by
Franklin Watts
96 Leonard Street
London
EC2A 4XD

Franklin Watts Australia
45-51 Huntley Street
Alexandria
NSW 2015

Always go for a walk with an adult. Take care around water.

Planning and production by Discovery Books Limited
Editor: Geoff Barker
Designer: Ian Winton
Natural history consultant: Michael Chinery
Language consultant: Helen Barden
Photographer: Chris Fairclough, including front cover

Additional photographs: Bruce Coleman: 17 (Kim Taylor), 19t (Jane Burton), 20 (Werner Layer), 21 (Andrew Purcell), 22 (Kim Taylor); FLPA: 23 (Roger Wilmshurst); Getty Images: 26 (Bachmeier); NHPA: 13 (LUTRA); PhotoDisc: 10, 11; Alex Ramsay: 27.

A CIP catalogue record for this book is available from the British Library

ISBN 0 7496 5919 X

Dewey decimal classification number: 577.63

Printed in China

Contents

I went to a pond and
this is what I found.

There were pink flowers
and trees on the banks.

Lots of bulrushes and long
reeds swayed in the breeze.

The pond was very quiet
and still.

I saw a bird standing on
one leg. It was a heron.

I heard a noise among
the reeds.

It was some ducklings quacking.

A goose moved in the long grass.

I saw some ripples in the water.
The circles got bigger and bigger.

A fish had come up
to the surface...
and gone back down
again.

cygnets

A family of swans
swam close to me.

The mother was
gliding along with her
seven cygnets behind her.

Close to the bank the water
was covered in water lilies.

A pond skater
was walking
across the pond.
It really did
walk on water!

There was something slimy
in the pond weed.

It was frogspawn.
The black spots are eggs.

They will turn into
tadpoles, then
into frogs.

I peered into the water
and saw a newt.

I saw a dragonfly nymph
catch a worm.

The nymphs live in the water
for a year or more. Then they
turn into adult dragonflies.

I looked up and saw a dragonfly land on a plant.

I looked down at the bank and saw some tracks in the mud.

They were badger tracks!

A grebe was sitting on
her nest on the pond.

When she moved,
I saw four big eggs.

What was that flash of
orange and blue?

A kingfisher
had caught
a fish.

It was starting to get dark now.
Time to go home for tea.

Can you find these in the book?

heron

swan

frog